Copyright © 2024 by Victoria J. Arnold

All rights reserved.

No portion of this book may be reproduced in any form without written permission from the publisher or author, except as permitted by U.S. copyright law.

Visual credit by iStock.com/CoffeeAndMilk

Hello

ADULTHOOD

By: Victoria J. Arnold

CONTENTS

DEDICATION 7

TERMINOLOGY YOU SHOULD KNOW 9

INTRODUCTION 11

HELLO ADULTHOOD 15

    Pursuit of the Wrong Career 17
    Maxed Out 27
    Unsolicited opinions 35

HELLO FRIENDSHIPS 41

    Unbalanced Friendships 43
    FRIENDSHIP BREAK-UP 47
    Don't Compare Yourself, Prepare Yourself 52

HELLO RELATIONSHIPS 59

    Heartbreak 60
    alone, but not lonely 70
    dating 76

HELLO GRATITUDE 83

ACKNOWLEDGEMENTS 89

DEDICATION

This book is dedicated to you.

Yes, you, the very person reading this book.

Maybe you're in your twenties, thirties, forties, fifties, sixties, seventies, or older.

It doesn't matter how old you are; what matters is that at one point, you experienced or are currently experiencing what it's like to navigate the beginning stages of adulthood.

You've had to learn from many mistakes. You questioned yourself and your purpose.

You've experienced trying to maintain your mental health, physical health, friendships, love, self-care, and identifying your purpose in this life.

Life has taken you through many ups and downs, bringing you to where you are today.

I'm so proud of you!

I dedicate this book to you, hoping that you will find parts of this book you can relate to and resonate with and that can encourage you.

Terminology You Should Know

Newbie Adults - Individuals aged 18-27 who are embarking on their journey in adulthood and establishing their place in the world.

Marinated Adults - Individuals aged 28-39 who have simmered in the essence of adulthood, soaking up life's flavor and reaching a deeper understanding of themselves.

Seasoned Adults - Individuals aged 40 and above who have matured like fine wine, embodying life experience and wisdom gained through their ongoing journey in adulthood. These individuals are not to be called "old"; they are seasoned with experience.

FYI: If you're 40 and above, the next time someone says you're old, make sure you tell them "I'm not old, I'm seasoned."

"**Life Be Lifing**" - A popular saying among millennials and generation Z; it implies that life continues to unfold, regardless of our plans or expectations.

Example: "*Life be lifing…I had an interview this morning and caught a flat tire on my way there.*"

Ghosting - Abruptly ending communication with someone without an explanation.

INTRODUCTION

Adulthood kicks off at the ripe age of 18,

where you proudly proclaim,

"I'm grown now!"

It's the crossroads after high school where the options linger:

"College, career, or forging your own path?"

Ultimately questioning if you're going to pursue your passion or pursue the expectations from your parents.

It's other people telling you how to live your life while you strive to find your voice.

It's applying for jobs in your field and being turned down because you don't have enough 'experience'.

It's the reality of financial responsibility.

It's learning how to budget with debt as an unwelcome companion.

And amid the chaos, new friendships form while some older friendships dissolve.

It's navigating the trenches of the dating scene, with heartbreaks and healing as obligatory chapters.

Adulthood, especially in the beginning, is a rollercoaster ride.

It is exhilarating and exhausting, where each twist and turn shapes us into

the resilient individuals we are destined to become.

GENTLE REMINDER:

Make sure you reviewed the "Terminology You Should Know".

Hello

ADULTHOOD

Pursuit of the Wrong Career

Unsolicited Opinions

Maxed Out

PURSUIT OF THE WRONG CAREER

I remember when I turned 18 years old and I was preparing to start college. I lost count of how many people said to me: *"Go to college, get a degree, and get a job with good benefits."*

And it was typically seasoned adults who would say this to me. I noticed that most of the seasoned adults who told me this did not go to college themselves. Or they went to college, and for some reason, they were unable to finish college. Then, there were some seasoned adults who went to college and got their degrees and jobs with benefits. So, I knew the speech, "Go to college, get a degree, and get a job with good benefits," from them was coming from a good place. I followed the advice of the seasoned adults in my life. I started by going to college. I majored in theatre and took several college classes I was passionate about, such as directing, writing, film, and acting. I loved college because I was studying and majoring in an area I was passionate about. Eventually, I went on to graduate and receive my degree in theatre.

After college graduation, I envisioned immediately starting a career in theatre or film. I submitted my resume to companies hiring for production crew members and auditioned for casting calls. Unfortunately, I was faced with a lot of rejections or no callbacks.

During this time, I was working at a retail store at the mall that paid me less than $14 per hour, and the hours were inconsistent. I needed a better job, so I also started applying for some office jobs. Eventually, I got a call back with a job offer. It wasn't from a production company or casting call. The job offer was from an insurance company, and you know what they offered? Good benefits such as health insurance, dental, vision, and 401K. Those were the things seasoned adults told me to have. So, I accepted the job and started working in a corporate office for an insurance company.

I did not realize it then, but when I accepted that job offer, I put my passion in the backseat. My passion for the arts was placed on the back burner while I worked a corporate job.

Can I be honest? I didn't like sitting at a desk. I didn't like staring at a computer screen all day or answering call after call and having to put on a fake voice for customers. I didn't like working corporate, and I never envisioned that I would ever be spending eight hours sitting at a desk doing something I didn't enjoy. But before I knew it, a little over 5 years went by, and I was still caught up clocking in at a job that paid me extremely well but left me drained and unfulfilled every day.

    I felt unfulfilled because I pursued the wrong career.

I settled for a career that disconnected me from my aspirations.

No matter how many promotions, raises, or bonuses my job gave, it still did not fulfill me. And now, as a 29-year-old woman, when I look back, I recognize it's because I wasn't doing something I loved. Sure, I went to college and majored in an area I was passionate about. However, I took a job that resulted in me placing my talent and passion in the backseat.

I've always had a feeling that my purpose in life was so much bigger than sitting at a desk, working a 9-5 job. I'm sure many of you reading this can relate to that feeling—the feeling that you are supposed to be operating in something different. I came across many co-workers who had been working in the same field or position for over 20 years. One of my co-workers in her late sixties would always say to me,

> "You're still young. You can find something you love to do. I'm going to retire soon, so I'm hanging in there."

I felt bad for my co-worker. I could not imagine myself working at a job for over 20 years that I didn't enjoy and staying around because I was approaching retirement. At this same job, I ended up writing a short role play for the team I worked with. My supervisor at the time shared what I wrote with the section manager. And one day, while I was at work, the section manager asked me to come to her office. I was nervous, because I've never been called to the section manager's office. When I walked in and sat down, she asked me *"Did you write the role play?"*. I nodded and answered yes. She was surprised because she didn't know I was a writer or had a background in performing arts. During our conversation she looked me in my eyes, and she said to me,

> "Victoria, I wish I could fire you so you can focus on doing things related to what you love."

I laughed it off, but what she said resonated with me.

My mother's best friend—I'll refer to her as 'Mrs. P'—would frequently text me and ask,

"Are you putting your dream to the test?"

She would also send me opportunities related to film and television productions. At first, I didn't see the point in why she continued to text me about that or send me production opportunities. But deep down, I needed someone to do that; it felt like a gentle reminder to ensure I didn't forget what I once wanted. The crazy part is that I never once told Mrs. P how unfulfilled I felt at my job and with the decisions I made career-wise as a young adult. But I thank God that it was in her spirit to keep texting and having those conversations with me.

It is so easy to get comfortable, complacent, and stuck in a 'work routine' when it comes to a career.

Think about it. Some of you may say:

"I don't like my job, but I've been working here so long. Why would I leave or do something different?"

Sometimes, becoming too comfortable and complacent can result in us lacking motivation to want better. It may also result in simply being scared to do something different. After working at the same place for over five years, I was the result of both.

I lacked motivation to want better for myself, and I was scared to do something different.

I needed to take steps to pursue more of what fulfills me. It was time to look in the backseat where I placed my talent and passion over five years ago; it was time to pick it back up. On a USB drive, I had several scripts for stage plays and ideas I had written over the years. They were scripts I wrote, saved to my USB drive, and never touched them again. I started back working on my scripts and new ideas that came to mind.

Directing and writing short plays for my church, New Macedonia Baptist Church, in Riverdale, GA, sparked a fire in me. One short play was for Black History Month, and the second short play was for Christmas. I felt excitement working with the cast, collaborating with audio and visual, and the musicians to bring the plays to life.

It was in those moments that I felt fulfilled because my talent was being exercised and used. I felt a sense of purpose along with joy. What I did came naturally. I didn't have to put on a fake voice like I did at my 9-5 job. I was able to show up as my authentic self. And in life, whatever we pursue, we should be able to show up as ourselves. We shouldn't feel like we have to talk a certain way, act a certain way, or be a different person to fit in.

> We should be able to show up as ourselves.

Oftentimes, our talent and passion are something we do naturally. Maybe you are a great singer, and people ask you to sing at events; maybe you are a great photographer, and people always ask you to take their photos—the list is endless. Your talent, along with passion, allows you to show up and use it naturally. Now if you don't mind me asking,

What are you passionate about?

I understand when you're younger, sometimes parents want you to be a doctor, nurse, lawyer, preacher, or maybe they want you to take over the family business.

But what do you want?

And how bad do you want it?

DISCLAIMER FOR PARENTS:

I encourage each of you to listen to your children when they express their passion, whether they want to study in college or would rather go to a trade school. Support your children's passion and stop telling them things like:

"You won't make a lot of money."

"That's nonsense. Find something else to do."

"That's not a real career."

If someone doubted your dream when you were younger, you shouldn't repeat the cycle and doubt your child's dream. Your child's passion may not always be your passion. And your child's dream may not look like yours; that's because God gave that dream specifically to them, not you. Encourage and support them in their heart's desire.

Now, back to your passion…

If you're going to work the majority of your life, why not work doing something you are passionate about, something that fulfills you?

Because when you're working for fulfillment, every day, you get excited about what you're doing.

So, if you're passionate about nursing and caring for sick people, go to school, study, get the certifications and go into the medical field. If you're passionate about doing hair or make-up, then find a good cosmetology school, get enrolled, get certified, and start beating people's faces *(FYI: the term 'beating a face' means doing make-up; we don't mean physically beating someone's face)*. If you want to start a business, identify your niche, what service your business will provide for others, and who your target customers will be. Read the books on entrepreneurship and take the classes.

Keep in mind that everyone's path is different. Your path is not going to be the exact same as your parents, your sibling, or your best friend. That's the beauty of adulthood; we all have different success stories and can learn something from one another to grow and succeed more.

If you are anything like I was, lacking motivation and feeling complacent with where you are right now…

Plant a seed.

Plant a seed of your passion.

I know some of you are saying, "*Plant a seed? What are you talking about? I don't want to start a garden!*"

Hear me out…

Plant a seed of your passion, and every day, do something to water your passion.

The seed of your passion that you are planting may be that business idea you keep thinking about. And one of many actions to water that passion could start by doing research, reading a book about entrepreneurship, brainstorming your logo design, or applying for an LLC. To see our passion grow, we must be consistent by doing something each day to water our passion. And remember, the water you put into your passion every day does not have to be something big or expensive. Many times, it starts by doing research.

It's not too late to plant a seed of your passion and water it. You don't have to wait 10-20 years to look back and say things like,

"I wish I would've started that business" or "I wish I would've taken that course."

You can start now.

There are too many of us out here not watering our passion. And I know there can be doubtful thoughts, such as:

"What if I don't succeed?"

"What if I don't get into medical school?"

"What if no one likes it?"

"What if my business idea fails?"

"What if I'm too old?"

But you deserve to look back over your life and say,

"I'm so glad I went after this!"

"I'm so glad I started this business!"

"I'm so glad I started this non-profit!"

"I'm so glad I applied to medical school!"

"I'm so glad I submitted my application or audition tape!"

"I'm so glad I didn't let my age stop me!"

Whatever you desire to do, you deserve to pursue it!

You deserve to look back over your life and be proud that you pursued your passion. You are capable, and God gave you that talent, passion, and vision for a reason. So plant a seed of your passion, and every day, do something to water your passion so that one day, you can look back to see growth and appreciate the effort you made to stimulate the growth.

Include Your Passion and Talent in Everyday Life

If we incorporate our passion and talent into everyday life, we can experience greater fulfillment and a sense of purpose.

1. Make time and be consistent.

Set aside time to engage in activities related to your passion or talent. Whether it's three days a week or maybe you can schedule 30 minutes to 1 hour every day, consistency is key.

By making the time and being consistent, we stay connected to what we love.

2. Stay curious.

Stay open-minded about your passion and talent; don't be afraid to try new things. Look for opportunities to grow and learn, whether it's through reading or connecting with others who take an interest in the same field.

3. Set goals.

Be specific and concise when setting a goal. This could involve learning a new skill related to your passion or talent, completing a website, attending a seminar, etc. When we define clear goals, we give ourselves direction.

4. Share it with others.

It's important to share our passion and talent with family, friends, or our community. Sharing our passion or talent with others can bring forth a sense of happiness and purpose.

MAXED OUT

Mentally and Emotionally

Financially

MAXED OUT

Mentally and Emotionally

We've all faced those moments when it seems like our minds and hearts are running on overdrive. It's like we are pushing the limits, trying to juggle too much at once. I've been there, feeling mentally and emotionally maxed out, as if I am lost in a sea of thoughts, feelings, and physical exhaustion crashing down all at once.

It took me a while to realize why I was constantly overwhelmed. The root of the cause? Always saying yes to others' requests for help, constantly putting their needs before my own. I realized that I was always rearranging my priorities to help others with their request. As a result, I would find myself struggling to keep my own head above water.

Every time this happened, I would go days leaving calls unanswered and texts unopened and completely silent on social media. Doing this resulted in some people who were so used to hearing from me asking if I was okay and if something was wrong. I started realizing that this wasn't a healthy solution. I knew I had to find a way to deal with the overwhelm without burning out completely.

It was time to figure out how to hit pause so it would not hit me too hard.

It wasn't easy, but I knew I had to make a change. Slowly, I began prioritizing myself, my needs, and my well-being. With time, I found a balance that allowed me to be there for others without sacrificing my own mental and emotional health or stretching myself too thin.

First, I had to learn that not everything could be accomplished all at once. Learning how to prioritize my tasks was important, acknowledging that some things would inevitably be left undone because I could not do everything at one time or in one day. This involved me breaking tasks down into smaller, more manageable steps, allowing me to focus on completing one thing at a time. By doing so, I found I could stay on top of things without feeling overwhelmed.

A good strategy I found was setting clear boundaries, which means learning to say no when necessary, without guilt or apology. Incorporating the word 'no' was a significant shift. I had to assure myself that it was acceptable to decline requests that drained my energy or added more to my plate than I could handle.

Another aspect was becoming more self-aware and having self-compassion. I had to have compassion for myself, acknowledge my worth, and understand that my needs mattered too. I had to learn to listen to my body, recognizing when I needed to rest, relax, or if I needed support or help. Instead of pushing through exhaustion or ignoring when I would physically feel tired, I allowed myself time to acknowledge what I felt and rest.

It also meant making time for self-care activities that replenished my energy and nurtured my soul. Some of my activities were taking part in hobbies that I loved like going to the nail salon or spa, buying new plants, decorating my house, etc.

> Taking a step back and allowing myself to take a break was essential. I needed to give myself permission to pause and recharge.

By doing all of these things, I was nurturing my well-being, and I began to have the capacity to show up for others from a place of abundance rather than depletion. Because there is no honor in exhausting myself or constantly putting my well-being and needs on the back burner. It's not a badge of honor to burn out or neglect myself.

> And the same goes for you; it is not a badge of honor to neglect your well-being and needs. Say it out loud to yourself,

"It is not a badge of honor to neglect my well-being and needs."

Taking care of ourselves isn't selfish; it is an important aspect of showing up fully in our own lives and for others. Just like we need to charge our phones to keep them running, we need to recharge ourselves to navigate through life. When we neglect our well-being, not only are we doing ourselves a disservice, but we also limit our capacity to support and uplift those around us.

Taking care of ourselves means recognizing that we deserve the same love, compassion, and care that we freely give to others and understanding that by nurturing ourselves, we're better equipped to implement positive change in our lives and those around us.

Prioritizing yourself doesn't mean neglecting others; it's about finding a balance that honors your needs and your relationships with others.

MAXED OUT

Financially

There were many times I found myself stretched financially. Let's be real, I'm not here to sugarcoat it or pretend that I've always had it together when it comes to money. I've stumbled, made mistakes, and learned some lessons along the way.

And I'm willing to bet I'm not alone. We've all got our share of financial regrets, those moments where we wish we could hit rewind and take a different path, armed with the knowledge we have now.

Typically, when we have a regret, we say things like, "*I wish I didn't do that,*" "*Why did I do that?*" or "*That was so stupid of me!*" Often, we immediately scold ourselves, which can turn into negativity. However, I'd like to challenge you to shift your mindset. Instead of thinking so harshly of your regrets, I challenge you to think about the lessons coming out of it.

My financial overwhelm started when I was 19 years old and I mistakenly got my first credit card. I know someone is asking, "*Victoria, how did you get a credit card by mistake?! And was it really a mistake?*"

Yes, I promise I got my first credit card by mistake. I went to the mall and went inside Victoria's Secret to get measured for a bra. When I went to check out, the sales associate asked me if I wanted to apply for the 'rewards program' and receive 20% off my purchase that day.

I said yes because all I heard was that I would receive 20% off my purchase. I love a discount; when you're a 'broke college student', you take all the discounts you can get. So, I signed up for the rewards program. I should've stopped when the screen prompted me for my social security number, but remember, I was 19, so I didn't think much of it. My mind was solely on getting 20% off my purchase. The next thing I knew, the sales associate told me I was approved for a $500 Victoria's Secret credit card.

I was shocked. I'd never had a credit card before. I didn't know what to do with a $500 credit card and I didn't know a 'rewards program' was code for a credit card. The sales associate asked if I wanted to put it on the card. And I said yes without hesitation because it meant I didn't have to spend the money I brought with me. I didn't have to use my money whenever I wanted to shop at Victoria's Secret.

It was that exact mindset that started the problem, thinking…

"I don't have to use my money whenever I want to shop at Victoria's Secret."

That mindset and lack of knowledge about credit caused me to make many mistakes. I made several purchases with no strategy or plan on how to make payments on my credit card. To make things worse, in the same year I opened two more credit cards with a bank.

And before I knew it, my three credit cards were maxed out.

I didn't have the money readily available to pay my credit cards off. I started getting phone calls and e-mails about my credit card account being past due. It was time for me to take control of my finances and make a commitment to pay my credit cards down in a timely manner. The situation ultimately forced me to acknowledge my spending habits so I could better manage my money. A lot of purchases I made were out of impulse. I had to start tracking my expenses to see where my money was going and ultimately asking myself *"Is this something I truly need to purchase right now, or am I buying this out of impulse?"*

So instead of saying, *"I regret having a credit card"*; now I say things like, *"I have experience with maxing out a credit card."* and *"I'm now better at managing money."*

Errors and mistakes shape us into better versions of ourselves.

In our journey of recovering from regret or mistakes, it is important to shift our focus from dwelling on the issue to embracing the lessons they offer. By shifting our mindset to focus on the lessons learned from our mistakes, we allow ourselves to become better overall.

Now, I look at mistakes as signposts that help direct us towards better strategies and better approaches. By acknowledging and learning from our own errors, we also become equipped to help others who may encounter the same problem. Rather than viewing our mistakes as setbacks or failures, we should see them as opportunities for development.

UNSOLICITED OPINIONS

I think it's safe to say that each of us has encountered unsolicited opinions and questions from others. You know, **when someone you didn't ask** speaks their opinion on what you should be doing with your life or where you should be in life. Sometimes, people's opinions, comments, and questions can feel intrusive and unwelcome.

Throughout my twenties, I dealt with constant unsolicited opinions from different people. In fact, I'm still dealing with unsolicited opinions. I want to be clear: it does not stop after you exit your twenties.

Unsolicited opinions from people are like flies in the summer, constantly buzzing in your ear.

Typically, unsolicited opinions and questions often come from people close to us. The majority of unsolicited opinions I received came from some of my family. It was constant opinions, comments, and questions such as:

"You need to get married."

"You should be getting married and have kids by now. I was married and had kids when I was your age."

"You need to go back to school for a master's degree."

"You should have a baby by now."

"When are you going to settle down?"

"When are you going to get married?"

"When are you going to have a baby?"

The constant opinions and questions were so exhausting that I honestly wouldn't even want to talk to certain people because, in every conversation, they would make the same comments or ask me the same questions. And the older I got, the more I continued to grow private and short with my answers.

I tried my best to be polite when responding to people who asked me the same questions over and over. But there was one instance when a specific person had the nerve to say to me, I should be done having kids by age thirty. I told that person,

"Stay out of my uterus!"

That's right, I said it...

"Stay out of my uterus!"

How rude it is to tell a young woman when she should be done having kids. I wasn't going to just have a baby to say, *"I have a baby."* And I certainly wasn't going to rush to get married just to say, *"I'm married."* I was not going to do things to meet a made up deadline people had for my life.

Isn't that funny?

Some people actually have a 'deadline' regarding when you should do things in **your life**.

And I used to let the comments, opinions, and questions from other people get under my skin. But let me tell you something: now I'm in a place where I set boundaries and no longer allow opinions or questions to get under my skin. By the time I reached my late twenties, I realized I did not owe anyone an explanation for my life. So, I started setting boundaries and responding to people's questions and opinions by saying things like,

"Thanks for asking, but I don't want to talk about that right now."

"I understand your perspective based on your life experience, but this is my life, and this is my experience."

"I know how things were done back then, but I prefer to do it this way in my life right now."

"Thank you for sharing, but I'm going to do this my way."

"I'm just not going to do that."

"You don't have to ask me the same questions every time we talk."

"If there's an update in my personal life, I'll tell you when I'm ready."

And if you're a woman…you might have to literally tell someone occasionally to "*Stay out of your uterus*" when they say insensitive comments about your age or childbirth. At the end of the day, none of your family or friends can live your life for you because it is your life to live.

Say it out aloud,

"This is my life to live."

It's important we do not allow the comments, opinions, and questions of others to undermine our sense of self-worth or direction in life. Everyone's journey is different, and what works for one person may not necessarily apply to another.

Often, opinions stem from individual perspectives and experiences that may not accurately reflect our own truth or aspirations. Rather than internalizing feedback from others, we can choose to filter it through a lens of discernment. This means we extract the good, constructive insight and we discard unwarranted, insensitive comments.

Remember, this is your life to live.

Hello

FRIENDSHIPS

Unbalanced Friendships

Friendship Break-ups

Don't Compare Yourself, Prepare Yourself

UNBALANCED FRIENDSHIPS

Friendships are a significant part of our lives. Typically, friends are one of the first people we go to when we need advice. Our friends are there when we want to share good or bad news, a secret, and when we need support or encouragement during difficult times.

The truth is, the older you get, the smaller your friend circle becomes. In my early twenties, I had a very large group of girlfriends, and I used to tell people that I had eight best friends. Today, I literally laugh out loud when I think about the times I told people I had eight best friends. During that time, I honestly thought anyone I was a best friend to was my best friend in return. As I matured, I noticed that in some of my friendships, the communication and initiations to hang out constantly fell on me.

Over time, I recognized that I was experiencing unbalanced friendships.

With certain friends, the only time I would see them was when I reached out to ask if they wanted to go out or to invite them to a party I would have. In return, sometimes certain friends would cancel on me last minute, or they were just never available to hang out when I asked them. Then, there were some friends that I only heard from when they had problems or were going through a tough time. They would make it a point to contact me and vent about their problems. After I would listen and give them words of advice, I would not hear from them again until they had another problem.

I'm sure some of you reading this have experienced an unbalanced friendship where it feels like you're doing most of the work to keep the friendship active. Recognizing when there is not a good balance in a friendship is important.

An unbalanced friendship may look like this:

- You're always the person who calls or texts first.
- The only time they call or text you is when they are facing challenges or need emotional support.

- A friend that consistently does not show up for you (ex., Milestones in your life, parties you invite them to, a new business adventure, etc.)

In today's time, many people are quick to completely cut off a person when this happens. Often, many people will cut a person off without trying to have a conversation first. If you value the friendship, I believe it's important to try at least to have a conversation about what you have noticed. I'm not saying a conversation will fix everything, but having a conversation is a good place to start.

It gives you the opportunity to be direct with expressing yourself and also allows your friend to understand why the friendship is not in a good place. If having a conversation does not resolve the issue and nothing changes, then you might need to consider taking a step back from the friendship. Unfortunately, not all unbalanced friendships can be saved and that's okay. If you have made the effort to have the conversation and you do not see any changes, it's healthy to move on.

I'll admit, there were some unbalanced friendships I couldn't save. Looking back, I realize friendship is a two-way street and it wasn't solely my responsibility to rescue every friendship.

Now I've come to deeply appreciate and cherish the balanced friendships in my life today. The friends that randomly call to catch up or initiate plans to hang out, check on me when they notice I've been quieter than usual, and show up in times of need. Those friends have taught me the true value of friendship and what a balanced friendship looks like in return.

FRIENDSHIP BREAK-UP

We often think that friendships with people we've known the longest will last forever. But sometimes your oldest friendships don't always last forever. Some of your oldest friendships come to an end, whether due to the natural course of growing apart or the occurrence of conflict, argument, or betrayal. The occurrence of a conflict, argument, or betrayal between two friends may result in a friendship break-up.

I honestly don't feel like there's enough discussion about friendship break-ups. When you've been friends with someone for years, it is tough to navigate a friendship break-up. I'm going to share my friendship break-up experience and how I dealt with it. I'll be referring to this person as "Mirage".

I was 23 years old when I went through a friendship break-up and I have known Mirage since we were small children. We were childhood friends that were very close, grew up going to the same church, singing in the choir together, and even hanging out outside of church.

One day, a mutual friend of ours personally told me that Mirage slept with someone I previously dated. Honestly, I didn't believe it, but the mutual friend told me they were 100% sure this happened. So, the next time Mirage and I hung out, I asked Mirage if it was true. Mirage answered no and assured me that she would never do anything like that. Mirage made me feel bad for even asking such a question.

I felt awkward because there I was, face to face with Mirage asking if this was true. And Mirage was very defensive, and adamant that it didn't happen and repeatedly denied such a thing.

So, I tried to let it go. I really tried to let it go.

But you know that little thing called 'intuition'? Well, I could not shake the feeling that Mirage was not being honest with me, and my intuition was telling me that Mirage was lying to me.

A few months later, I ended up having a general conversation with the guy I used to date, and at one point I was direct by asking him if this happened. And very solemnly, he answered yes. I was silent once he answered the question and abruptly ended our conversation. To be honest, this situation took me to a place where I read both of them for filth and I cursed both of them out. If you know me, then you know I don't cuss. I'm very polite and understanding, but this situation took me completely out of my character. Although I received apologies from both of them; I couldn't just 'be cool' with them again.

I was most hurt by my 'friend'. Because Mirage played in my face by doing that, and continuing to hang out with me, and lying to me. We couldn't bounce back from that situation, and it ended our friendship. Mirage was one of my oldest friends and cutting her off was tough. One of the hardest parts of a friendship break-up is adapting to life without your friend. That means no longer calling them or talking on FaceTime, finding old photos you've taken over the years, the weirdness of still knowing their birthday even though you no longer speak, and the awkwardness of occasionally crossing paths in familiar places, and driving past their neighborhood where you once spent a lot of time hanging out.

While friendship break-ups can be painful, I don't believe we're meant to forget the person who was once our friend. Even when a friendship has ended, the memories shared, and lessons learned from the friendship remain a part of our journey.

It can be challenging to move forward from a friendship break-up, especially a friendship that lasted for years and meant a lot to you. I will share a few things I did during the time my friendship with Mirage ended.

Acknowledge how you feel.

There are often a lot of emotions that come when a long-time friendship comes to an end. I tried to sweep my emotions under the rug and put on a tough shell. But the truth is I was hurt by what happened. Acknowledging how you feel is always a good place to start.

Distance yourself, even on social media.

Although Mirage and I were no longer friends, I kept Mirage as a friend on my social media pages. But eventually, I made the decision to remove her from all my social media because we were literally not friends in real life. Therefore, we did not need to stay connected on social media or view what was happening in the other's life going forward.

Hitting that 'unfriend' or 'unfollow' button after a friendship break-up is like decluttering your online space to make room for positivity.

Stay connected to positive friendships; don't isolate yourself.

After the friendship break-up, I isolated myself from the rest of my friends. But I had two friends who kept reaching out to me because they wanted to make sure I was okay. I noticed that I felt better after talking to the friends I still had. Although I lost a long-time friend, I recognized that I still had genuine friends that were trying to be there for me. So, I didn't need to isolate myself from my friends. I needed to embrace the friendships I still had.

Staying connected to positive friendships is important. Surrounding ourselves with supportive and uplifting individuals can provide encouragement, which reminds us that we are not alone; we are valued and appreciated for who we are.

Sometimes ending a friendship can be a bittersweet reminder of personal growth. It takes courage to acknowledge when a friendship is no longer serving a healthy balance.

DON'T COMPARE YOURSELF, PREPARE YOURSELF

Have you ever compared yourself to a family member, a friend, or a social media influencer?

You know, feeling like you're behind because of what you see those around you have accomplished. Oftentimes, we may see those around us do things that we feel like we should also be doing, especially if they are in our age group. Maybe the person we're comparing ourselves to is buying a house, running a successful business, getting married, or having a baby.

When we compare ourselves to others, we often compare their current results to our results because results are what we see when we look at another person's success. We often do not see the efforts or failures that happened before they reached success.

Think about it…

We see someone with a successful business, but we don't see how they financially struggled for years to get their business off the ground. We don't see the challenges they faced paying their bills every month. We don't see the time the business almost went bankrupt. And we don't see how that person almost gave up on their dream of owning that particular business.

We see someone buy a beautiful home. What we don't see is how they lost all their belongings, whether it was in an eviction, a fire, or a flood. We don't see how long it took that person to get back on their feet. We don't see the amount of struggle they had to go through before they bought a house.

We see a person get engaged and get married. Often, we don't see how many failed relationships and heartbreaks that person experienced before they met their soulmate. We don't see all the cheating and the abuse they went through in their last relationship. We don't see many times that person gave up on love.

We see someone have a baby, but we don't see how long they struggled with infertility issues before they had a successful pregnancy. We don't see the miscarriage(s) that person had. We don't see the tears and the amount of time they spent praying and simply hoping for a healthy pregnancy and delivery.

Typically, we don't see the process a person went through to get to where they are today.

I purchased my first house when I was 27 years old. A lot of my family and friends only saw the result, which was me purchasing a house. No one saw the ups and downs in finding and buying a house.

I put in several offers on houses that I absolutely loved. Several sellers declined my offer and decided to go with an investor who was offering cash. It happened many times to me, and I started doubting if homeownership was meant for me. I almost gave up. But for every 'no' I got, I started looking at it as additional time to prepare even more. I read books about how to budget and manage my finances. I kept working overtime at my job every week. I continued reminding myself that I was equipped to buy a house and that I was in position to receive a house.

And a small voice kept telling me, "*Every no is just bringing you closer to the YES.*"

So instead of saying to myself, "*When will a seller accept my offer?*" or "*When will I be able to close on a house?*"

I shifted my thoughts to:

"*Let me prepare myself for the YES.*"

Eventually, a seller accepted my offer. And the closing worked in my favor because the seller paid my closing cost! On top of that, I also ended up getting a check from the seller.

Can you believe that?

I walked away from the closing table with money.

I already saved up a substantial amount of money to prepare myself for the closing and any additional costs. But the unexpected blessing that the seller paid my closing cost and I still received a check from the seller in the end was more than I could have asked for!

You see, I just wanted to hurry up and buy a house.

We often just want stuff to happen, and we're not mentally, physically, financially or spiritually prepared to **receive** what we say we want. We have to prepare ourselves for when it's our turn to receive what we're asking for.

It's so important that we are prepared to receive what God has for us and what we ask of God. It's kind of like having a baby. I know some of you are saying, "Now, how is this like having a baby?!"

Just hear me out...

There is still a level of preparation parents must do before a baby is born. Parents must prepare themselves for a baby by selecting a doctor, packing a hospital bag, making sure the baby's car seat is installed properly in the car, etc. Many first-time parents may even take a parenting class to ensure they know what they are doing when the baby is born.

But it may not be marriage or kids that you want right now. Maybe it's a business you want to start, and you want the business to make a lot of money and be successful like the businesses you see on social media. Well, you've got to prepare yourself for it to happen! Take the entrepreneur workshops or classes, do the research, attend seminars, take the time to learn and understand how to manage money for your business, watch YouTube videos, and study other business owners.

The preparation to receive what you want starts before you get it. Because if you're not **prepared** for what you're asking for, you will mishandle it when it comes your way. And the last thing you want to do is fumble a blessing!

When trying to achieve a goal or progress in a specific area in our lives, it is inevitable to encounter some 'no' and rejections along the way. But it is important to remember that every no and every rejection brings us one step closer to the 'yes' that we seek and the goal we are working to accomplish. Instead of being discouraged by the 'no', let's embrace every no as stepping stones on the path toward our 'yes'.

The no, the setbacks, and the rejections are your stepping stones toward the yes, so keep on stepping.

Prepare yourself because that YES you're waiting for is on the way!

Hello

RELATIONSHIPS

Heartbreak

Alone, But Not Lonely

Dating

HEARTBREAK

We all have experienced heartbreak in one form or another, whether it is hurt from a romantic relationship, from a family member, or from a friend.

My heartbreak experience came from a relationship I was in during my twenties. Throughout this portion, I'll be referring to this guy as "Camouflage". Like most people, I fell in love in my twenties, and I was certain that the relationship I was in would result in marriage. It was something we talked about and something we both wanted.

Camouflage and I were in a long-distance relationship. He lived in South Carolina, and I lived in Georgia. I went to South Carolina, and he'd also come to Georgia to make our relationship work. I met some of Camouflage's family, and he also met some of mine in return.

Camouflage and I discussed many things. We discussed career goals, personal struggles, issues in our past, marriage, and kids. Being long-distance, it was important that we establish which state we wanted to live in together since the long-term goal was to marry one another. Camouflage expressed his desire to move to Georgia.

Like any relationship, it had its tough moments. The fact that we were in a long-distance relationship made it more challenging. We had to consistently plan when we would see each other and during this timeframe, two years went by. After a year and a half, Camouflage had still not moved to Georgia, and I didn't see his efforts in preparing to move. I didn't hear him talk much about moving a lot anymore. I noticed it was me having to bring it up to him.

I always checked in with him, asking if this was what he still wanted. Every time, he would say yes and constantly reassure me that he was still serious about being together and moving to Georgia. He told me he was just working on transferring his job to a location in Georgia and I believed him.

One day, Camouflage told me he had lost his job. I was there for him, checking on him and trying to encourage him. Shortly after he told me that he lost his job, Camouflage completely stopped talking to me. He stopped answering my calls and responding to my texts. At first, I thought he was hurt or something happened. I really thought something was wrong.

Nothing was wrong. He just ghosted me.

Days of him not returning my calls or texts turned into weeks, and weeks turned into a month. After a month went by, I stopped trying to contact him altogether. His silence was loud and very clear; he did not want to talk to me. And I did not know why. I felt confused and lost. We used to talk every day throughout the day; he was the first person I spoke to every morning and the last person I always said good night to. I've never been ghosted before, and this hurt.

I spent a lot of time trying to make sense of it. I was trying to move forward from a relationship with no closure. I was struggling with this. So, I decided to find a therapist, and she was instrumental in helping me through the odd space I was in and prioritizing my emotional well-being. While going to therapy was helping, I still thought about him every day.

A few months later, I opened my Instagram as I typically do throughout the day. And on this particular day something told me to check Camouflage's Instagram. I saw Camouflage posted a new photo. The photo was of him down on one knee proposing to another woman. When I saw his Instagram post, I was in shock more than anything. There it was in my face. Deep down, I suspected there was someone else, but I didn't want to believe it.

It hurt really bad.

Real, real bad.

I started questioning everything he ever said to me or told me. And I started to feel angry. I was so angry that I shut down. I immediately canceled all my upcoming therapy sessions; I didn't want to talk about it. I was hardly answering my phone or replying to texts. And I didn't even leave my house for three days. I just wanted to sit in my feelings alone.

Although I was angry and hurt, I was still level-headed enough to know that I didn't need 'payback' and I didn't need to go on social media and embarrass him or publicly call out my ex for what he did. One thing I knew for sure, is that we reap what we sow. So I cried, I prayed, and I asked God to help my heart not be hardened.

Eventually, I wrote Camouflage a very long message expressing my feelings, and I sent it to him. After I sent the message I blocked him. I stopped trying to be strong about the situation. I had no choice but to acknowledge how much this hurt me. It was in that moment I realized, "*I actually **can't** deal with this on my own.*"

Let's be honest: when you experience significant hurt, it can turn you into a cold, mean person towards other people. Hurt and anger started to fester in me. I was constantly thinking every man would lie to me, cheat on me, and hurt me. I was slowly becoming bitter, and I was too young to be bitter. I didn't want to feel like this for the rest of my life.

I didn't want to grow old and say things like, "*I'm this way because of what my ex did 20 years ago.*"

I wanted to release the hurt. I wanted to reach a place where I could truly move forward, but I didn't know where to start or where to go. Where do you start when there's so much hurt and anger built up inside?

It started with me.

I had to do the work within myself.

Frequently, people experience pain within relationships, family dynamics, or friendships. And instead of addressing it, people attempt to bury it by rushing past the discomfort without doing the necessary reflection and healing.

There were three major areas within myself that I needed to acknowledge and address:

1. Letting go of things that hurt me
2. Holding a grudge
3. Forgiveness

I already knew I struggled with all three for a while, but this situation with Camouflage intensified it. And I didn't want to carry hurt and grudges into my next relationship. I certainly didn't want to carry it into a marriage one day. I didn't want to walk around with hurt and unforgiveness in my heart for the rest of my life.

I didn't want the bitter version of me.

I wanted a better version of me.

To reach the better version of me, I had to do the work within myself and work on those three areas in my life.

Now let me ask you,

Have you done the work within yourself?

It's never too late, and you're not too old to do the work within yourself. Maybe the situation that hurt you happened 1 year ago or 20 years ago. No matter how much time has passed, you don't deserve to walk around carrying the weight of that hurt for the rest of your life.

You are worthy of letting go of the things that have hurt you, you deserve to release your grudge, and you are capable of the ability to forgive.

Letting go means letting it out.

If you shake a Coke bottle or soda can enough when you open it, it fizzles up and explodes. The same thing can happen to each of us if we do not release how we feel in a healthy way.

Letting it out may look like finding outlets such as talking to someone, journaling, crying to help release that pressure, or reading something encouraging that relates to your situation. It can be scary to talk about how a situation affected us, especially if you're not the type to talk about how you feel.

But if we suppress our emotions, it can lead to a build-up of pressure, just like shaking a Coke bottle, and eventually, if not released, those emotions can explode in unexpected ways.

For me, I eventually decided to go back to therapy. I needed an outlet to talk about the emotions I felt and sort through them.

Holding a grudge is like carrying a heavy object.

If you're going to hold a grudge, you might as well pick up the heaviest object you can find and carry it around for 24 hours every day. Carrying heavy objects can weigh us down physically, just like holding a grudge weighs us down emotionally and eventually mentally or physically. Holding a grudge requires effort and it's a constant reminder as to why we are upset or angry. Just like carrying around a heavy object is a reminder of what we are holding onto.

At some point, it starts to feel heavy. I felt the weight of the grudge I was holding against my ex.

The weight of holding my grudge didn't bring me any relief, especially when I tried to move forward and date. I didn't realize that I was carrying it around with me in the form of anxiety (anticipating the situation to repeat itself again), constantly questioning if a man was being truthful with me and dealing with trust issues that often resulted in me lashing out unnecessarily toward the wrong person.

To be honest, holding a grudge doesn't bring any of us a resolution or relief. It prolongs our suffering while the person we're holding the grudge against has likely moved forward. I've learned that we cannot hold on to our hurt forever. Because if we do, we risk bringing anger and resentment into new relationships and friendships.

Forgiveness is not easy, but it's freeing.

When I reached a place of forgiveness towards my ex, I felt free. I felt free of the hurt I was carrying with me, free from the anger and resentment I once felt.

I want to be very clear; it took me a long time to forgive.

I realized that forgiveness does not mean we have to bring the person back into our lives, it doesn't mean we have to return to the situation that hurt us, and it doesn't mean that we have to act like nothing happened.

But this situation taught me that I, in fact, had to acknowledge what happened in order to take a step forward. Forgiveness entails recognizing the situation or individual that caused us pain, along with the bitterness or resentment we harbor towards them and ultimately releasing the emotional burden we carry within us.

You are worthy of releasing the weight of the grudge you've been carrying. Doing so doesn't diminish the significance of what occurred, nor does it display weakness. It reflects strength and bravery to step away from the heaviness of past hurt. It may not happen all at once. It's okay if it's a gradual process, releasing the emotional burden piece by piece until you're liberated from its weight.

Over time, I took sticky notes and wrote down the things I was holding a grudge against, the things I wanted to let go of. I wrote it in pen. Pen is permanent, just like the things that happen in our lives are permanent and we cannot erase them.

Some days, I had one sticky note, and other days, I had two or three sticky notes. But with every sticky note, I wrote down the thing I wanted to let go and release, I said a prayer over each one, and I laid it down in the trashcan. I tied the trash up and took it completely out of the house to the garbage bin to be carried away.

That was my method of releasing my grudge and hurt. I shared that to highlight a process I used to release my grudges and hurt. By no means did I do all of this in one day; it took a long time. When we carry grudges and hurt with us, we may have to lay them down and release them one by one, just like I did with each sticky note. But you don't have to do the exact same thing I did. Your release may look different from mine. Your past hurt may also look different from mine.

If you're walking around with past hurt, I know it's heavy, and it's okay for you to set it down now, even if it's piece by piece. Each one of us deserves to be free from past hurt.

Don't give up on freeing yourself from the weight of the hurt.

ALONE, BUT NOT LONELY

In my twenties, I learned how to be alone without feeling lonely. This season allowed me to self-reflect, connect with myself more, and ultimately strengthened me to appreciate myself.

There is a difference between being alone and lonely. Being alone is a state of being, such as simply being on your own or in a state where you're currently not with another person or with a group of people. In comparison, being lonely is more of an emotion and/or a feeling associated with sadness or missing something.

I went through a season of being alone, but not lonely.

Alone time gave me the confidence to do small and big things outside of my comfort zone. I became confident walking into a party or an event by myself where I only knew one person or no one at all. I know this may seem small.

But let me tell you, I used to NEVER walk into events or parties alone. I used to be so nervous to walk into an event or a party alone. Before my alone season, I would sit in my car and wait for someone I knew to arrive so we could walk inside a party together. I was even nervous to start a conversation with people I didn't know.

My friend and I had tickets to attend a small business mixer. We agreed to meet each other at the venue. I got there first, and as usual, I waited in my car until my friend got there. After waiting for a while, she called me and told me she was having issues with her car and wouldn't be able to make it. She said to me,

"Go ahead and go in!"

All I kept thinking about was how I didn't know anyone there and how awkward it was going to be the entire time. I was in downtown Atlanta, and I really contemplated driving back home to avoid going to the event alone, where I knew no one. Then I thought about how expensive gas is, my make-up and how much time I spent making sure it looked good, my outfit, and how cute I looked overall. I didn't drive all the way here dressed up to turn around and go home. I was nervous, but I made the decision to walk in alone.

As soon as I walked in, a woman walked right up to me, welcomed me, and showed me around. Then she walked away, and I was by myself, looking around a room full of people I didn't know. Then I thought to myself, *This is only awkward if I make it awkward.* So I grabbed a cocktail, sat down at a table with others, and started a conversation by asking everyone's name. From there, it took off, and we talked about many things like our professions, hobbies, stuff happening on social media, etc. By the time I left the event, I had met two people who hugged me and told me goodbye. It felt like we were friends. I remember getting in the car and feeling shocked that I went to an event alone. I know that may seem small to someone else, but considering I never go anywhere alone, it was a big deal for me.

I started enjoying being alone more. I embraced taking my first solo trip. That's right, I took a flight to Florida to go to the beach…alone. And I had so much fun! You see, I've always gone on group trips, which means there's typically an itinerary, and you have to wake up with everyone else to do the things the group wants to do.

But on my solo trip, I was free to do simple things like sleep in or wake up early. I rented a beach cabana and sat alone on the beach all day, sipping my drink while reading a book. And no one was there to interrupt me and say, "I'm ready to go back to the hotel room," or ask, "How much longer do you want to be out here?" I embraced the opportunity to enjoy my solo trip without interruptions.

I embraced living alone. I embraced moving into my own place, decorating, and creating a home. My great-aunt Lillie knew, and I visited with her often before she passed away. My great-aunt Lillie was so excited for me. I remember when she said to me,

"Livin' on your own, good for you, baby!".

She told me she didn't know what it was like to live alone until she was 87 years old when her husband, my great-uncle Archie, passed away in 2020. Aunt Lillie decided to live in her house alone in her eighties, and she embraced it.

There are some people who think there is something wrong with being alone. Some people think they constantly have to do things with another person or with a group of people. And I'm breaking that narrative to say…

You don't.

It's okay to step out and do some things alone.

The things I did alone resulted in me gaining a deeper appreciation for myself. And an even greater appreciation to have company and to spend quality time with the people I love.

I understand that it's not easy for some people to be alone, and being alone may scare some of you. If so, I challenge you to ask yourself why.

Why does being alone scare you?

It could be because you've never been alone before and you don't know what to do with yourself. Or it could be because you associate being alone with a traumatic experience you've had in your life. And maybe it's time to address that trauma.

I don't know the answer to why you may be scared of being alone. Only you can answer it. All I ask is that you be honest with yourself.

And I understand it can be challenging to do. But it can also be so freeing to be honest with yourself. And when you're alone, you don't have to be in a state of "constant production", meaning you don't have to always be productive when you're spending time with yourself.

Sometimes it's just about being present in the moment and enjoying the moment.

Moments that are simple but impactful. Such as watching a movie with a bag of popcorn by yourself. You don't have to share any of your popcorn, snacks, or drinks with anyone else because you're alone. And in that very moment, you're laughing really loud at the movie, and you realize how much you're enjoying the time to yourself.

Maybe you're home alone, blasting your music on the speakers while you clean up. You're singing aloud and dancing while you clean. And in that very moment, you realize how much you're enjoying the time to sing obnoxiously loud and dance by yourself with no one watching you.

Maybe it's bigger, like planning a solo trip to a place you've never been. And in that moment, you're on your solo trip eating really good food, or you're touring the city. You realize the amount of joy you have while you're on your trip.

You're enjoying being present in the moment you're in.

I want to encourage newbie adults, marinated adults, and seasoned adults who experience a phase of loneliness to shift their perspective to…

Alone, but not lonely.

And begin to embrace the alone time to yourself. There is so much strength and growth that comes when we embrace where we're at.

DATING

Dating is just like a rollercoaster ride; it's seeing that attractive, thrilling ride at the amusement park and feeling that rush of excitement and nervousness. It's getting on and experiencing the highs and lows as we hold on with the hope of making it to the end. As we date, sometimes we find ourselves clinging to the safety bar, bracing for the unexpected twists or turns and the occasional jolt of disappointment.

But overall, we tend to uncover layers of both ourselves and others, as each encounter offers new insights and lessons. I was fortunate enough to date a lot throughout my twenties. Dating allowed me to discover values that were important to me and in return, helped me along the way in identifying if a man was a good fit for me. I discovered important qualities I wanted in a partner and qualities I did not want in a partner. Dating also showed me that 'good looks' aren't everything because sometimes 'good looks' are just 'good looks' with no substance.

In my dating journey, I learned when it was time to move on. There was a man I spent a considerable amount of time with, and our connection felt promising. However, my fear of scaring him away with too many questions held me back from expressing my true desires. I desired a committed relationship that would lead to marriage. It took me some time to work up the courage to discuss my hopes for a committed relationship. When I finally brought up the topic of a committed relationship, he told me that he wasn't ready for a relationship.

And it was hard for me to accept what he said to me. It was hard for me to accept it because I was invested before ensuring we were on the same page. I invested my time with this man. And time is so important, because it is something I could not get back.

I was disappointed that I was just finding out he was not ready for a relationship, disappointed that I invested time, and disappointed that I waited so long to ask him questions about what mattered to me. Ultimately, we were not on the same page. I desired a relationship and he did not.

Unfortunately, I had already developed strong feelings for a man that was not ready to move forward. I owed it to myself to stay true to what I desired; I owed it to myself to not settle. It wasn't easy, but I had to let him know that I could not continue spending the amount of time we were spending together.

If you've been in the realm of dating, chances are you've heard these infamous lines:

"*I'm not ready for a relationship.*"

"*I don't know what I want.*"

"*I'm not over my ex.*"

"*Let's just have fun and see where this goes.*"

I've come across all of these during my own dating experiences, and if someone has said one of these lines to you, it's important to take their words at face value. There's no need to decipher or read between the lines because these statements are straightforward. You shouldn't feel obligated to wait around, prove yourself, or try to change someone's mind. Trust what they're telling you and honor your own needs and boundaries.

Communication is key, but so is listening to our intuition. If a person expresses hesitancy or reluctance to commit, pay attention to their words and actions. Trust your gut instincts, and don't ignore any red flags that may arise. Don't compromise your values or settle for less than you deserve out of fear of being alone. Remember that walking away from a situation that doesn't align with your needs is an act of self-respect and self-love.

When you're dating, don't be afraid to ask questions early and often.

Asking questions early reduces the possibility of experiencing a devastating disappointment in the long run. Asking questions early and often brings forth clarity for both individuals. It can clarify whether you and the other person are on the same page or not. The last thing you want is to be with someone for months or years, then ask them, "When do you want kids?" only for them to tell you they don't want any children. And that might be a deal breaker for you.

On the other hand, maybe it's not about kids. Maybe you've been with someone for a long time, and you start asking questions about marriage to find out they do not believe in marriage or want to marry.

Don't wait until you've spent countless time together to ask questions about what matters to you.

Unfortunately, when we are met with disappointing answers or results many of us will look at all the time we invested with a person. We look at all the days we spent with someone, the trips we took, the money we spent, and the gifts we purchased. Sometimes, we do so much for someone before ensuring we are on the same page regarding what we want and what matters most. That's why I encourage anyone dating to ask the important questions early and often. Because it's never too early to make sure you're on the same page with the person you're dating.

Sadly, there are some people who find themselves stuck in unhealthy relationships or situation-ships longer than they should out of fear of starting over. I've had friends open up to me about this fear and admit they know their relationship or situation-ship is not healthy, but they're hesitant to walk away and start over. I am quick to remind them that if they decide to walk away, they are starting with experience. With each dating encounter we develop more knowledge and instincts to recognize and avoid certain pitfalls we experienced before.

I know we live in a world where timelines and expectations may dictate our decisions, resulting in rushing through the dating process. Sometimes, we set artificial deadlines for ourselves, hoping to achieve certain milestones by a certain age. For example:

"I want to be married by 25 or 27."

"I want to date someone for two years, and by the third year, we have to get engaged."

"I want to be done having children by age 30."

Rushing to meet a self-imposed deadline can lead us down the wrong path, which may result in regretting our decisions and prevent us from finding a genuine connection with another person.

So, for anyone who may feel the weight of accomplishing self-imposed deadlines, it's okay if you don't always meet every timeline you set. The best moments come unexpectedly, often reminding us that timing is beyond our control. So embrace the process, stay open to the unexpected, and trust that the right moments will find you when the time is right.

Hello

GRATITUDE

As I approached the milestone of leaving my twenties behind and stepping into my thirties, a wave of nervousness came over me. I tried to make light of it by joking with my friends about whether thirty would hurt or not. But making jokes did not relieve the nervousness I felt. I had to ask myself, *What exactly am I nervous or scared about?*

It wasn't the number 30 itself that made me anxious, but rather the uncertainty that comes with aging. The unknown aspects of what lies ahead and the inventible changes that come with time are the things that made me feel anxious. Focusing on the uncertainties felt overwhelming, and it was starting to take away from my ability to enjoy the present.

I wanted to shift my focus to thankfulness and gratitude for where I'm at today.

And also the things I have learned, accomplished, and overcome throughout the decade of my twenties. It was time for me to embrace gratitude and view aging in a different light.

Embracing gratitude means embracing every stage of life, including the process of aging. Instead of fearing getting older, I'm learning to welcome it with open arms, recognizing that with each year comes wisdom and opportunity for growth.

Getting older is like leveling up in a video game; we unlock new skills and abilities along the way. With each level, we gain more strength, courage, knowledge, and understanding. I've learned that aging is simply an ongoing journey of self-discovery where every birthday is a cause for gratitude and celebration, with each year bringing us closer to our truest selves.

When we enter a new decade, we often think about the changes and what might unfold. We wonder what puzzle will be presented in front of us to solve as we age. And the uncertainty of the puzzle's difficulty level can make us feel anxious.

But I believe every birthday is a moment to reflect on the challenges we've overcome, the lessons we've learned, and the progress we've made. By doing so, we honor ourselves and reaffirm our worth. It's a reminder that we made it through another year. No matter how old you are, it's important to honor your journey and resilience each time you make another trip around the sun.

Each of us deserves to enjoy the present and embrace gratitude.

As you turn this final page, I hope that something in this book has sparked a fire within you, reminding you of your strength and potential and leaving you encouraged.

- Victoria J. Arnold

ACKNOWLEDGEMENTS

To my parents, Joe and Valarie Kay Arnold,

I am so grateful God chose both of you to be my parents. I would not be the woman I am today without you two.

Although my mama is no longer physically with us, her influence continues to shape the woman I am today. From a young age, I learned invaluable lessons in kindness, patience, and compassion by simply observing her interactions with others.

Because of her example, I strive to embody the same qualities in my own life, honoring her legacy and the profound impact she had on shaping the woman I've become.

My dad has been my rock since day one, always cheering me on and reminding me of my potential. His constant encouragement, belief in my abilities, and reassurance that I can achieve anything I set my mind to have fueled me to keep going even when things got tough.

The encouragement he has poured into me has not only shaped my journey but also influenced me to pay it forward by inspiring and uplifting others in return.

No matter how old I get, my hope is to always make my parents proud.

Made in the USA
Columbia, SC
23 June 2024

fa8b7049-4ba2-450f-b50e-44e8e9601ee7R02